Collins

INTERNATIONAL PRIMARY ENGLISH

Progress Book 1

Student's Book

Published by Collins

An imprint of HarperCollins*Publishers*
The News Building, 1 London Bridge Street, London, SE1 9GF, UK

HarperCollins*Publishers*
Macken House, 39/40 Mayor Street Upper, Dublin 1, D01 C9W8, Ireland

Browse the complete Collins catalogue at
www.collins.co.uk

© HarperCollins*Publishers* Limited 2023

10 9 8 7 6 5 4 3 2 1

ISBN 978-0-00-865479-5

British Library Cataloguing-in-Publication Data
A catalogue record for this publication is available from the British Library.

Author: Daphne Paizee
Series editor: Daphne Paizee
Publisher: Elaine Higgleton
Product manager: Holly Woolnough
Project manager: Just Content
Copy editor: Tanya Solomons
Answer checker: Karen Williams
Proofreader: Catherine Dakin
Cover designer: Gordon MacGilp
Cover illustration: Petr Horácek
Typesetter: David Jimenez
Illustrator: Ann Paganuzzi
Production controller: Lyndsey Rogers
Printed and bound in Great Britain by Martins the Printers

With thanks to the following teachers for reviewing materials in proof and providing valuable feedback: Sylvie Meurein, Nilai International School; Gabriel Kehinde, Avi-Cenna International School; and with thanks to the following teachers who provided feedback during the early development stage: Najihah binti Roslan, Nilai International School.

MIX
Paper | Supporting responsible forestry
FSC
www.fsc.org
FSC™ C007454

The publishers gratefully acknowledge the permission granted to reproduce the copyright material in this book. Every effort has been made to trace copyright holders and to obtain their permission for the use of copyright material. The publishers will gladly receive any information enabling them to rectify any error or omission at the first opportunity.

Cambridge International copyright material in this publication is reproduced under licence and remains the intellectual property of Cambridge Assessment International Education

This text has not been through the Cambridge International endorsement process.

Contents

How to use this book 4

I can statements 5

Unit 1 Going places 12

Unit 2 Having fun 18

Unit 3 Let's find out 24

Term 1 Test 30

Unit 4 The moon 34

Unit 5 *Funny Fish* 40

Unit 6 Food 46

Term 2 Test 52

Unit 7 Traditional stories 56

Unit 8 Feelings 62

Unit 9 Life lessons 68

Term 3 Test 74

How to use this book

This book is full of questions. Each set of questions can be completed at the end of each week.

The questions allow you to practise the things you've learned. They will help you understand topics that you might need more practice of. They will also show you the topics that you are most confident with. Your teacher can use your answers to give you feedback and support.

At the end of each set of questions, there is a space to put the date that you completed it. There is also a blank box. Your teacher might use it to:

- sign, when they have marked your answers

- write a short comment on your work.

Date: _____

Now look at and think about each of the *I can* statements.

Pages 5 to 11 include a list of *I can* statements. Once you have finished each set of questions, turn to the *I can* statements. Think about each statement: how easy or hard did you find the topic? For each statement, colour in the face that is closest to how you feel:

☺ I can do this   ☐ I'm getting there   ☹ I need some help.

There are three longer termly tests in the book. These can be completed after each block of units.

I can statements

At the end of each week, think about each of the *I can* statements and how easy or hard you find the topic. For each statement, colour in the face that is closest to how you feel.

Unit 1 Going places	Date:		
Week 1			
I can read short words.	🙂	😐	☹️
I can draw a picture and talk about it.	🙂	😐	☹️
Week 2			
I can find words that rhyme.	🙂	😐	☹️
I can put sentences in the right order.	🙂	😐	☹️
I can tell a story.	🙂	😐	☹️
Week 3			
I can say the alphabet in order.	🙂	😐	☹️
I can find information in pictures.	🙂	😐	☹️
I can talk about things I like.	🙂	😐	☹️
Unit 2 Having fun	Date:		
Week 1			
I can read a story.	🙂	😐	☹️
I can answer questions about a story.	🙂	😐	☹️
I can read and write sentences.	🙂	😐	☹️
Week 2			
I can read high frequency words.	🙂	😐	☹️

I can spell words that rhyme.	🙂	😐	☹️
I can make a list.	🙂	😐	☹️
I can use capital letters to write names.	🙂	😐	☹️
Week 3			
I can use lower case letters and capital letters in sentences.	🙂	😐	☹️
I can spell words with *sh*.	🙂	😐	☹️
I can talk about and read a story aloud.	🙂	😐	☹️
I can act in a role play.	🙂	😐	☹️
Unit 3 Let's find out	**Date:**		
Week 1			
I can find information in pictures and book covers.	🙂	😐	☹️
I can read words with *ng* and *ck*.	🙂	😐	☹️
I can ask and answer questions.	🙂	😐	☹️
Week 2			
I can read the contents page of a book.	🙂	😐	☹️
I can find information in a fact file.	🙂	😐	☹️
I can use pictures to help me read new words.	🙂	😐	☹️
I can write sentences with capital letters and full stops.	🙂	😐	☹️
Week 3			
I can write a caption about a picture.	🙂	😐	☹️

I can use pictures with labels to write sentences.	☺	😐	☹
I can read and recite a poem.	☺	😐	☹
I can make a list.	☺	😐	☹
Term 1 Test	**Date:**		
I can find information in pictures and book covers.	☺	😐	☹
I can read a book with information and answer questions.	☺	😐	☹
I can write sentences with capital letters and full stops.	☺	😐	☹
Unit 4 The moon	**Date:**		
Week 1			
I can say the alphabet in order.	☺	😐	☹
I can talk about a story and write answers to questions.	☺	😐	☹
I can make a shopping list.	☺	😐	☹
Week 2			
I can spell words with four letters.	☺	😐	☹
I can use common words.	☺	😐	☹
I can listen and write what I hear. (dictation)	☺	😐	☹
I can write a message on a card.	☺	😐	☹
Week 3			
I can tell a story in order.	☺	😐	☹
I can read a short poem aloud and answer questions about it.	☺	😐	☹

I can write about what I like in sentences.	☺	😐	☹
Unit 5 *Funny Fish*	**Date:**		
Week 1			
I can answer questions about a title page.	☺	😐	☹
I can write sentences with information.	☺	😐	☹
I can use sounds I know to read words.	☺	😐	☹
Week 2			
I can make a list of words that rhyme.	☺	😐	☹
I can write sentences I hear correctly.	☺	😐	☹
I can write sentences with information.	☺	😐	☹
I can spell common words correctly.	☺	😐	☹
Week 3			
I can make new words.	☺	😐	☹
I can copy, read and recite a poem.	☺	😐	☹
I can write a simple poem.	☺	😐	☹
Unit 6 Food	**Date:**		
Week 1			
I can draw and label pictures to give information.	☺	😐	☹
I can write a list of seafood.	☺	😐	☹
I can write sentences about fish and seafood.	☺	😐	☹

Week 2			
I can write rhyming words.	🙂	😐	☹️
I can write sentences with full stops.	🙂	😐	☹️
I can write facts about fruit and vegetables.	🙂	😐	☹️
I can draw a story map.	🙂	😐	☹️
Week 3			
I can write different texts for an information book.	🙂	😐	☹️
I can talk about foods I eat and enjoy.	🙂	😐	☹️
I can speak clearly and present information.	🙂	😐	☹️
Term 2 Test	Date:		
I can find information in pictures and book covers.	🙂	😐	☹️
I can read a traditional story and answer questions.	🙂	😐	☹️
I can write sentences with capital letters and full stops.	🙂	😐	☹️
Unit 7 Traditional stories	Date:		
Week 1			
I can write sentences that I hear.	🙂	😐	☹️
I can use *the* and *a* in sentences.	🙂	😐	☹️
I can answer questions about a story.	🙂	😐	☹️
Week 2			
I can spell some words with *ee*, *oa* and *ai*.	🙂	😐	☹️

I can read and write common words.	☺	😐	☹
I can put events in a story in order.	☺	😐	☹
Week 3			
I can read and write instructions in order.	☺	😐	☹
I can listen to a traditional story and suggest a new ending.	☺	😐	☹
I can make a story map.	☺	😐	☹
Unit 8 Feelings	**Date:**		
Week 1			
I can complete sentences with verbs that end in -ed and -ing.	☺	😐	☹
I can add full stops, question marks and exclamation marks to sentences.	☺	😐	☹
I can write answers to questions.	☺	😐	☹
I can read a story aloud with expression.	☺	😐	☹
Week 2			
I can read and spell words with oo, ee and ow.	☺	😐	☹
I can write sentences I hear.	☺	😐	☹
I can make a story map with captions and retell a story.	☺	😐	☹
Week 3			
I can read information in a fact file.	☺	😐	☹
I can answer questions.	☺	😐	☹
I can say what I think.	☺	😐	☹

Unit 9 Life lessons	Date:
Week 1	
I can write a list with a heading.	😊 😐 ☹️
I can read part of a story and answer questions.	😊 😐 ☹️
I can write words in order to make sentences.	😊 😐 ☹️
I can use capital letters.	😊 😐 ☹️
Week 2	
I can find nouns and words that rhyme.	😊 😐 ☹️
I can write sentences with 'and'.	😊 😐 ☹️
I can write an invitation.	😊 😐 ☹️
Week 3	
I can write a story.	😊 😐 ☹️
I can give my ideas about stories.	😊 😐 ☹️
Term 3 Test	Date:
I can listen to part of a story and write a new ending.	😊 😐 ☹️
I can read a story and answer questions.	😊 😐 ☹️
I can write sentences with capital letters and full stops.	😊 😐 ☹️

1 Read the words. Circle the word for each picture.

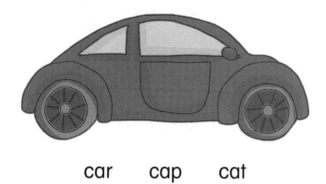

car   cap   cat

bed   boat   bag

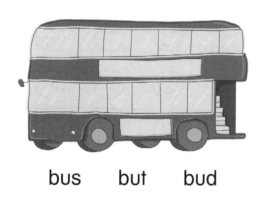

bus   but   bud

pet   bed   red

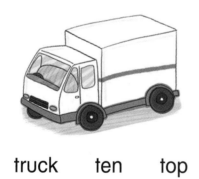

truck   ten   top

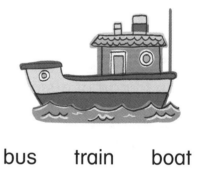

bus   train   boat

nut   but   put

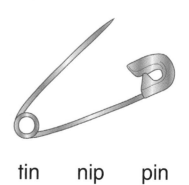

tin   nip   pin

2   Listen to your teacher and draw.

- Finish the drawing of the truck.
- Copy the name on the truck:

  The Red Truck

- Colour the truck.
- Draw a road.

3   Talk about your picture with a partner.

Look at and think about each of the *I can* statements.

Date: _____

1 Which words rhyme? Say the words. Make lists of the words that rhyme.

net	sat	hat	van	ran	bun	mat	fun	mop
man	hop	tin	in	top	bin	wet	sun	get

sat	man
_____	_____
_____	_____
run	top
_____	_____
_____	_____
tin	wet
_____	_____
_____	_____

2 Read the sentences in the box. Write a sentence under each picture.

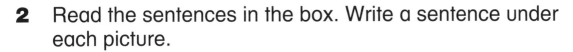

We go to Nut Hill.   I hug Grandpa.   I sit at the top.   I get on the bus.

_____

_____

_____

_____

_____

_____

_____

_____

3 Tell the story to a partner.

- How does the story begin?
- What happens after that?
- How does the story end?

Look at and think about each of the *I can* statements.

Date: _____

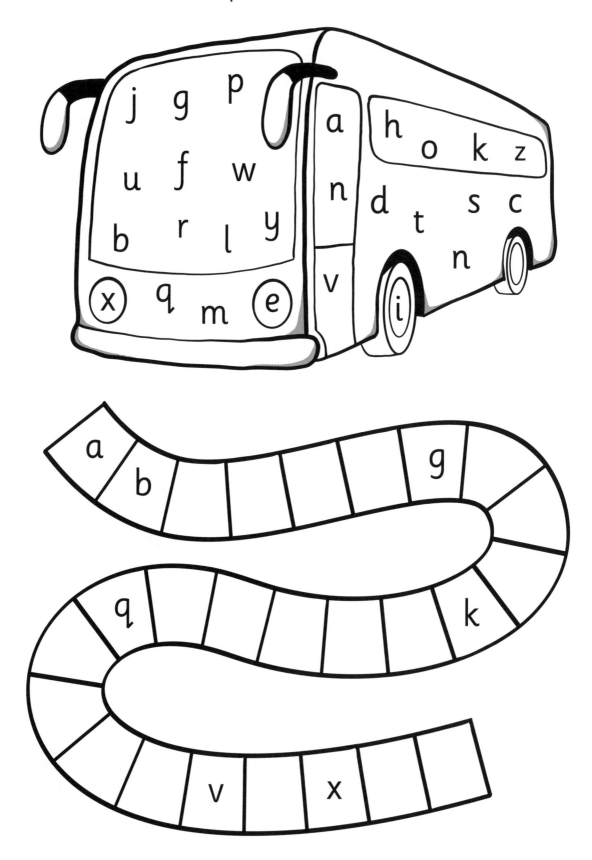

1   Write the letters of the alphabet on the track in the correct order.

2   Say the alphabet. Use the letter names.

3 Look at the pictures. Complete the words.

h __ t   __ e n   __ __ t   m __ g

4 Look at the pictures. Tick the correct answers.

1    **2**    **3**

a What is the title of the book in picture **1**?

☐ *Pam Naps*   ☐ *Pam and the Cats*

b Which book is a story?

☐ *Up and Off!*   ☐ *Pam Naps*

c Which book gives information?

☐ *Up and Off!*   ☐ *Pam Naps*

d What can you buy at the shop in picture **3**?

☐ books   ☐ bags

5 Which book would you enjoy? Talk about it with a partner.

_____

Look at and think
about each of the
I can statements.   ☐

Date: _____

1 Look at the pictures. Talk about what you see with a partner.

2 Read the story aloud with your partner.

Pam and Sam

Pam said to Sam, "I like to sit."
Sam said to Pam, "I like to be fit."

Sam said to Pam, "Look at me!"
Pam said to Sam, "Yes, I see!"

"You can run and jog," said Sam.

"I can hop on one leg and hop on the log!" said Pam.

Said Sam to Pam, "Yes, you can have fun."

Said Pam to Sam, "And then I can sit in the sun!"

3 Answer the questions.

a What are the names of the characters in the story?

_____   _____

b Can you find these words in the story? Circle the words.

| and | said | me | you | yes | have |

c What can you do to get fit? Make a list.

To get fit

hop

_____

_____

4 Look at each picture. Read the sentences. Underline the sentence that matches the picture.

a

He is jumping.

He is jogging.

b

They are reading.

They are cooking.

c

She can ride a bike.

She is swimming.

d

He can run fast.

He can hop and skip on one leg.

5 Draw a picture about something you can do.

Write a sentence about your picture.

Date: _____

Look at and think about each of the *I can* statements.

1 Read the words in the box. Use the words to complete the sentences.

said	and	the	you

a I can jog _____ hop.

b "We can have fun," _____ Pam.

c Can _____ show me?

d Pam is sitting in _____ sun.

2 Read the words aloud. Find words that rhyme from the story *Pam and Sam* on page 18.

bun   sun

am   _____

fit   _____

fog   _____

see   _____

peg   _____

3 Choose three letters of the alphabet. Make lists of names that begin with the letters.

S			
Sam Sanjeev Sandi			

4 Tell your partner what Pam and Sam can do.
Use these words:

run   hop   sit   jog   fun

5 Draw pictures of the words.

A word that rhymes with **fox**.

A word that rhymes with **wag**.

Look at and think
about each of the
I can statements.

Date: _____

1 Copy the sentences.

a I can run and hop on one leg.

_____

b My name is Rev.

_____

c Dev has a fish and a frog.

_____

2 Spell the words.

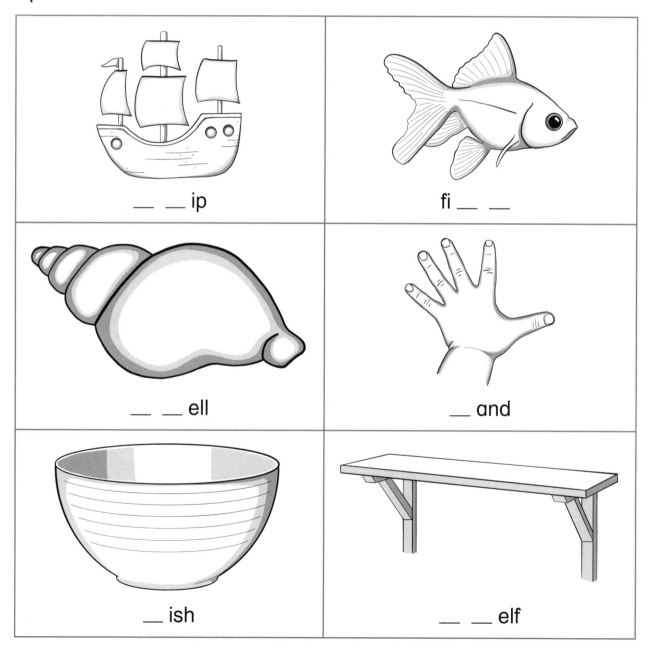

__ __ ip

fi __ __

__ __ ell

__ and

__ ish

__ __ elf

3   Write lower case letters or capital letters.

Write lower case letters	Write capital letters
A a	E e
T ___	___ d
M ___	___ f
G ___	___ h
Y ___	___ i
B ___	___ m
K ___	___ r

4   Say the alphabet in order.

5   Talk about stories you have read.

   a Which one do you like? Write the title.

_____

   b Why do you like the story? Tell a partner.

   c Act a scene from the story.

6   Choose part of a story. Read it aloud to a partner. Use actions.

Look at and think about each of the *I can* statements.

Date: _____

1 Talk about the covers with a partner. Tick the boxes for the correct answer.

a What will you find in these books?

☐ stories   ☐ information

b In which book can you find out about baby chicks?

☐ *Odd Fish!*   ☐ *Chick to Hen*

c What do you think *Odd Fish!* is about?

☐ Fish that look odd   ☐ How to count fish

d Which book would you like to read?

☐ *Odd Fish!*   ☐ *Chick to Hen*

2 Read the words aloud. Circle the words that rhyme.

a (neck)   (peck)   pick

b sing   song   ring

c sock   sick   lock

d duck   dock   luck

e pack   back   pick

f dish   wish   ding

3 Look at the pictures. Read the labels. Ask and answer questions about the pictures. Take turns with a partner.

Duck

beak

neck

wing

feet

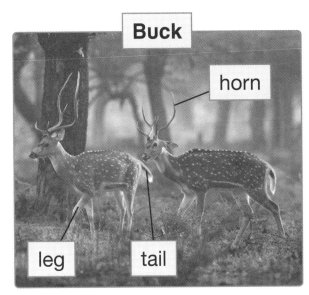

Buck

horn

leg

tail

4 Make words with the letters. Write the words.

a sock

_____

_____

_____

_____

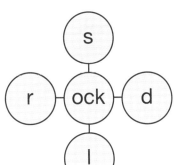

s

r — ock — d

l

b _____

_____

_____

_____

k

r — ing — w

s

Look at and think about each of the *I can* statements.

Date: _____

25

1 Read the contents page of a book.

All About Camels

Contents

Camels	2
Where camels live	3
What camels eat	4
What camels can do	5

2 Answer the questions. Write your answers.

a What is the book about?

_____

b On what page will you find out where camels live?

_____

c On what page will you find out what camels eat?

_____

d What will you find out about on page 5?

_____

3 Read the fact file about camels.

This camel cow lives in the desert with its calf.

FACT FILE:
Camels

Camels have long eyelashes to keep the sand out of their eyes.

Camels graze on plants.

Camels can carry people and things.

4 Answer the questions.

a Where do camels live? _____

b What do camels eat? _____

c What can camels do? _____

Look at and think about each of the *I can* statements.

Date: _____

27

1 Write a caption for the picture. Use some of the words in the box.

| frog | small | big | eyes | feet | four | two |

2 Look at the picture. Read the labels. Write two sentences about camels.

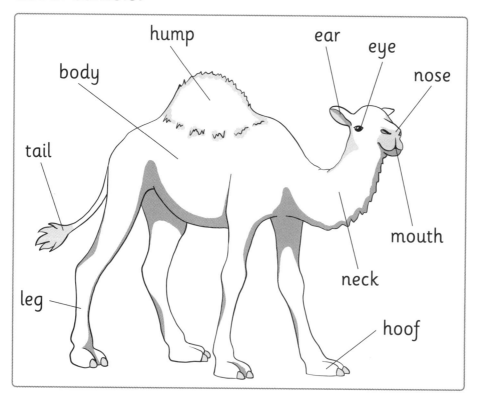

3 Read the poem.

4 Write the words from the poem that rhyme with these words.

roof _____

_____

boat _____

_____

blue _____

_____

My Goat

My goat is on the roof
Going *tap tap* with its hoof!

Now my goat is in my boat
And it's wearing my coat!

Now it has something blue.
Oh no! It's eating my shoe!

5 Look at the picture. What part of the goat is the hoof?

_____

6 What did the goat do? Tick three sentences.

☐ The goat went on the roof. ☐ The goat put on a coat.

☐ The goat ate a shirt. ☐ The goat ate a blue shoe.

7 Learn the poem and say it aloud to a partner.

8 Make a list of animals that live on farms.

goats

_____

_____

_____

_____

Date: _____

Look at and think about each of the *I can* statements.

☐

29

1 Look at the cover of this book. Tick the correct answer to each question.

a What is on the cover?

☐ two bear cubs ☐ two baby chicks

b What are cubs?

☐ baby animals ☐ farm animals

c Where do the animals in the picture live?

☐ in a forest ☐ in a river

d Is this book a story or does it give information?

_____

e Who wrote the book?

_____

f What do you think this book is about? Write a sentence.

_____

2 Read the book *Cubs*.

This fox cub has a log den.

den

This cub naps.

big cat

This cub gets a fish.

fish

This cub is hot.

This cub has a long sip.

It is fun to be a cub!

3 Answer the questions about *Cubs*.

a Where does a fox cub live?

_____

b Where can a lion cub nap?

_____

c What can a bear cub catch in the water?

_____

d What kind of animal is the cub on the rock on page 32?

Tick one box.

☐ tiger ☐ cheetah

e How do cubs play? Tick one sentence.

☐ They push and hug each other. ☐ They sip water.

f Complete these words from the story with *ck, sh* or *ng*.

ro __ __   pu __ __   lo __

4 Draw a picture of an animal you like. Write a sentence about the animal.

_____

Date: _____

Look at and think about each of the *I can* statements.

☐

1 Work with a partner. Take turns to say the letters of the alphabet in order.

 a b c

2 Look at the pictures from the story *Bot on the Moon*. Use the pictures to talk about the story.

3 Answer the questions.

a Where did Bot go?

_____

b What did he get at the Moon Shop?

_____

c What did he hit with his golf club?

_____

d What did Bot lose on the Moon?

_____

e This is a story. Is it true?

_____

4   Read the labels in the shop window.

5   Choose three things you want to buy at this shop. Write a shopping list.

Shopping list

_____

_____

_____

Look at and think about each of the *I can* statements.

Date: _____

1 Label the pictures. Use the words from the box.

flag   crab   mask   lamp   club   brush

_____   _____   _____

_____   _____   _____

2 Read the words in the box. Use the words to complete the sentences.

his   the   it   He   and   the

Bot ran up a hill on _____ Moon.

_____ hit _____ moon rock with _____ club.

Bot let go of his club _____ he lost _____.

3 🎧 Listen and write the sentences you hear.
Audio 1

a _____

b _____

c _____

d _____

4 Bot wrote a postcard
to his mum.
Read it aloud.

5 Make your own postcard from a place that you like.

a Draw a picture of the place.

b Write a message on the card.

Date: _____

Look at and think
about each of the
I can statements.

1 Use the story map to tell the story of *Bot on the Moon* to a partner.

2 Write sentences. Use the pictures to help you.

The _____ is on
a _____.

She can _____ in the sea.

We _____ and play on
our holiday!

They see the _____ in
the sky.

3 Read the poem aloud.

4 Answer the questions.

    a Find the rhyming words in the poem. Write them here.

    moon

    _____

    _____

    me

    _____

    b Find a sentence with a capital letter and a full stop in the poem. Copy it here.

    _____

    _____

    _____

    _____

    c Does the person who wrote the poem like the Moon? Why do you think that?

_____

5 What do you like more, a story or a poem about the Moon? Say why you like it.

_____

My Friend the Moon

My friend the Moon

tonight – a big yellow balloon

You watch me.

And you follow me.

Yes – I see!

Goodnight, Moon.

See you again soon.

Unit 4 The moon

Look at and think about each of the *I can* statements.

Date: _____

1 Look at the title page. Write your answers to the questions.

Written by Michaela Morgan

Illustrated by Jon Stuart

a Who wrote the book?

_____

b What are the fish doing?

_____

c Is it a story or an information book?

_____

d What is it about?

_____

e Look at the shape at the top of the fish. What is it, a big shark or a small fish?

_____

2   Read the words in the box. Use the words to make a list to describe the shark.

red	big	swish	bright	bad
scary	spotty	funny	stone	shy

The shark

_____

_____

_____

3   Write a sentence about the shark. Use words from your list.

_____

4   Draw a picture of two fish. Colour in the picture and label it.

Write a sentence with information about the fish. You can use the words in the box to help you.

tail	fin	eyes	head	body	mouth
	big	small	spotty	funny	

_____

Look at and think about each of the *I can* statements.

Date: _____

1 Complete this list of words that rhyme with "right".

br _____

l _____

n _____

m _____

2 Use two of the words you made to complete the sentences.

a I switch on the _____ at night.

b The Sun is not very _____ today.

3 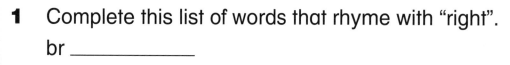 Listen and write the sentences you hear.

a _____

b _____

c _____

d _____

4 Colour in the pictures. Use two colours for each picture. Complete a sentence about each picture.

The flower is _____ and _____.

The bird is _____ and _____.

5 Complete the sentences. Use the correct word.

a Three _____ were swimming in the sea. (fish, fast)

b "I am the best fish here," _____ the red fish. (side, said)

c "I look _____ a stone," the funny fish said. (like, lick)

d A big fish _____ and ate the red fish. (came, game)

e That _____ the end of the funny red fish. (wash, was)

Look at and think about each of the *I can* statements.

Date: _____

43

1 Join the letters of the alphabet, then say them aloud, in order.

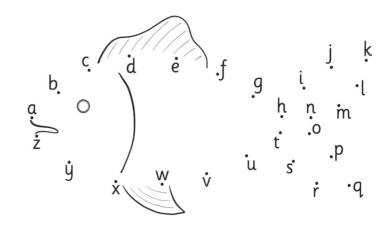

2 Change the first letter of each word to make a new word. Use one letter from the box for each new word.

| f | s | l | b | m |

Word	Letter	New word
dish	f	fish
bin		
go		
coat		
light		

3 Count the items. Complete the captions. Add a number word that begins with the same letter of the alphabet as the other words. Read the captions aloud.

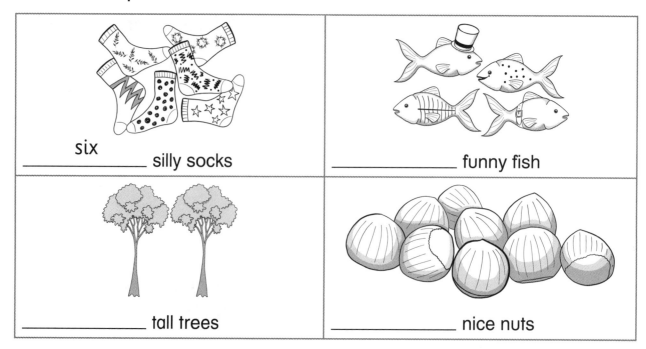

_____ six _____ silly socks

_____ funny fish

_____ tall trees

_____ nice nuts

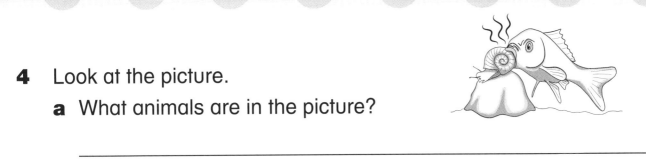

4 Look at the picture.

   a What animals are in the picture?

   _____

   b What is the fish doing?

   _____

5 Now complete a poem about the picture. Use rhyming words from the box or your own words.

snail	well
smell	today

Not today!
A fish with a red tail
Saw a huge grey _____

The fish bit the shell
But did not like the _____

So it swam away
Saying "No, not _____

As you can tell
I'm not feeling _____"

6 Copy a silly poem that you like. Write it neatly. Then say the poem aloud and tell a partner what it is about.

_____

_____

_____

_____

_____

_____

_____

Look at and think about each of the *I can* statements.

Date: _____

1 Write the names of the foods under the pictures. Use words from the box.

| orange | milk | fish | octopus | tomato | bread | sweet |

Fruit and vegetables

Bread and cereal

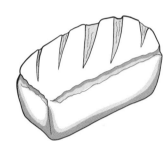

_____

Fish and seafood

_____

Dairy and eggs

a _____

Sugars and fats

a _____

an _____

a _____

an _____

2 Draw a line from each food to its food group.

3 Make a list of four seafoods. Choose four words from the box.

crab   banana   lobster   oyster   tuna   carrot

Seafood

_____

_____

_____

_____

4 Draw a picture of a food that is in the fish and seafood group.

   a Label your picture. Think about the size, colour, legs and body.

   b Describe your picture to a partner.

   c Write three sentences about your picture. Add a full stop at the end of each sentence. Start like this:

   This is _____

   It has _____

   _____

Look at and think about each of the *I can* statements.

Date: _____

1 Say each word. Then write two more words that rhyme.

brass _____ _____

press _____ _____

spill _____ _____

cross _____ _____

sell _____ _____

2 Draw a picture of a fruit or vegetable that you like.

a Label the parts of the fruit or vegetable.

b Write two sentences with facts about the fruit or vegetable in your picture.

_____

_____

3 Complete the sentences. Use the words in the box.

stone   leaf   and   a   root   An

Fruit _____ vegetables are plants. They are tasty and healthy.

_____ avocado is _____ fruit. It has a green skin and a big _____ inside.

We eat different parts of plants. Spinach is a _____ vegetable and we eat the _____ of a carrot.

4 **a** Make a story map with drawings to show how we get cheese.
   b Tell a partner about your story map.

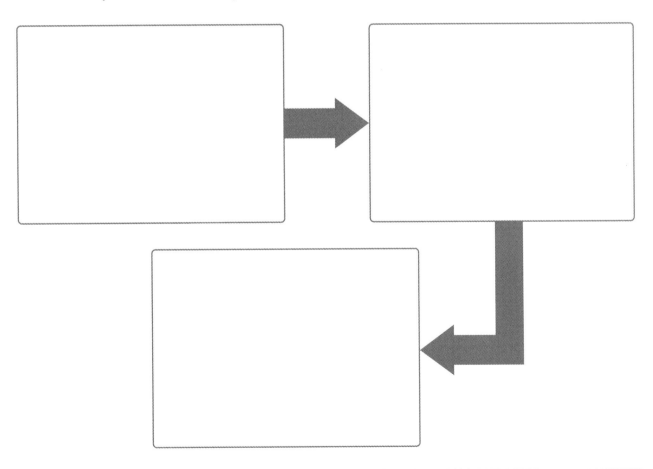

Look at and think about each of the *I can* statements.

Date: _____

1 Make lists. Choose three words for each list from the box.

| pitta | rice | eggs | jam | biscuits | chocolate | naan |

Sugars and fats

_____

_____

_____

Bread and cereals

_____

_____

_____

2 Make a cover for a book about food.

a Write a title.

b Draw or paste in a picture.

3 Write a contents list for the book.

Contents

_____

_____

_____

_____

_____

4 Choose one food that you like to eat. Give information about the food.

- Draw a picture.
- Label the picture.
- Write two sentences with facts.

5 Write instructions for making a food that you enjoy eating.

How to make _____

_____

First _____

_____

Next _____

_____

Then _____

_____

Last of all _____

_____

6 Present your pages to a partner. Talk about your book. Say why you enjoy the food.

Look at and think about each of the *I can* statements.

Date: _____

1 Look at the cover of this book.

a What does the picture on the cover show?

_____

b Where does the animal in the picture live?

_____

c Is this book a story or does it give information?

_____

d Who wrote the book and drew the pictures?

_____

_____

e What do you think this book is about? Write a sentence.

_____

2 Read the book *Red Hen*.

3 Answer the questions about *Red Hen*.

   a What did Red Hen have? Tick the correct answer.

     ☐ a puff of wheat   ☐ a bag of grain

   b List four jobs Red Hen did. The first one has been done for you.

     dig

     _____

     _____

     _____

   c Who are the characters in this story? Circle the names.

     Cat   Goat   Hen   Duck   Rat   Dog   Cow

   d Did the animals help Red Hen with her jobs?

     _____

   e What did Red Hen make?

     _____

   f The animals did not eat the buns. Why? Tick a sentence.

     ☐ They were not hungry.

     ☐ They did not help Red Hen to make the buns.

   g Complete these words from the story with letters from the box.

     ai   ff   ck   ll

     lu __ __   gr __ __ n   pu __ __   mi __ __

4 Draw a story map of *Red Hen*. Show the jobs that Red Hen did when she got the grain.

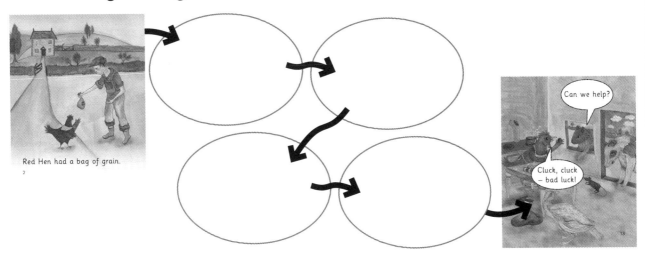

5 Write these sentences about the story in the correct order.

Then she plants the grain seeds.

Last of all she makes big jam buns.

The seeds grow big.

She mills the grain.

First she digs the soil.

Red Hen cuts the stems of the plants.

_____

_____

_____

_____

_____

_____

6 Tell the story to a partner.

Look at and think about each of the *I can* statements.

Date: _____

1 Write a word to match each picture.

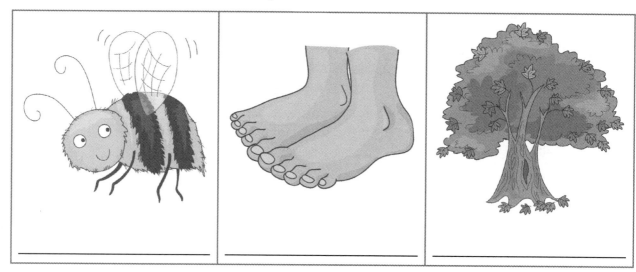

_____ _____ _____

2 🎧 Audio 3 Listen and write the sentences you hear. Then read your sentences aloud.

a _____

b _____

c _____

3 Complete the sentences. Use the words in the box.

the   a   The   a   the

a _____ small bun met

_____ cunning fox by

_____ river.

b I can see _____ bee

on _____ pink flower.

4 Read aloud the pages below based on the story *The Small Bun*.

 A man made a small bun.	 The small bun hopped off the dish and ran away.
 The small bun met a sheep. "Lunch! Yummy-yum!" said the sheep.	 Then the small bun met a goat. "Stand still! I will eat you!" said the goat.

5 Answer the questions.

a Who made the small bun?

_____

b Why did the bun run away? Tick the correct answer.

☐ It did not want the man to eat it.　　☐ It was not hungry.

c Who said, "Lunch! Yummy-yum!"?

_____

d Who said, "I will eat you!"?

_____

6 Read the story aloud. Use your voice and hands to show how the characters feel in the story.

Look at and think about each of the *I can* statements. ☐

Date: _____

1 Fill in the missing letters. Read the words aloud.

ee   oa   ai

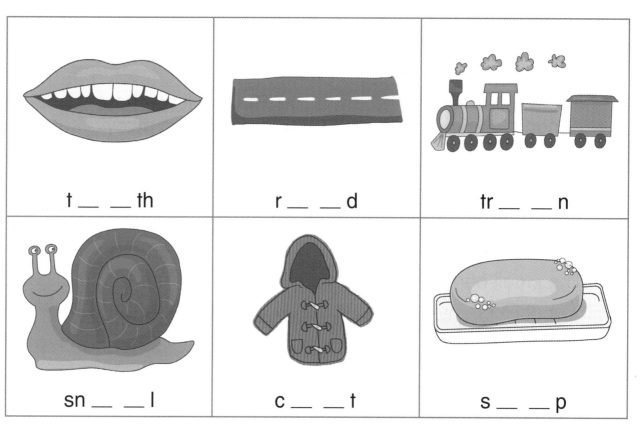

t __ __ th	r __ __ d	tr __ __ n
sn __ __ l	c __ __ t	s __ __ p

2 🎧 Audio 4 Listen and write the sentences you hear. Then read your sentences aloud.

a _____

b _____

c _____

3 Complete the sentences. Use the words in the box.

my   you   the   me   said

"Get on _____ back and I will carry you across the river,"

_____ the fox.

"If I get on your back, _____ will eat _____," said the

bun to _____ fox.

4   Look at the pictures from the story *The Small Bun*.

Read the sentences about the story. Write them in the correct order.

Next the bun met a cunning fox.

The fox ate the small bun.

The small bun hopped off the dish.

Then the bun met a hungry goat.

First the bun met a sheep.

_____

_____

_____

_____

_____

Look at and think
about each of the
I can statements.

Date: _____

1 Read the recipe for eggs on toast.

Eggs on toast

Ingredients

3 eggs

butter

3 big spoons of milk

3 slices of bread

Method

- Heat the pan.
- First mix the eggs with the milk.
- Then put the butter in a pan.
- Make toast with the bread.
- Put the egg mixture on the toast.
- Next cook the egg mixture in the pan.

2 Write the recipe instructions in the correct order.

_____

_____

_____

_____

_____

_____

3 🎧 Listen to a traditional story about a
Audio 5 lion and a mouse.

4 Answer the questions.

a Who are the characters in the story?

_____

b What was the lion doing? Tick the correct answer.

☐ sleeping ☐ eating

c Did the lion eat the mouse?

_____

d What happened to the lion? Tick the correct answer.

☐ He was stuck in a net. ☐ He was stuck in the mud.

e What did the mouse do?

_____

5 Suggest a new ending for the story.

6 Make a story map of *The Lion and the Mouse*.
Tell a partner about your story map.

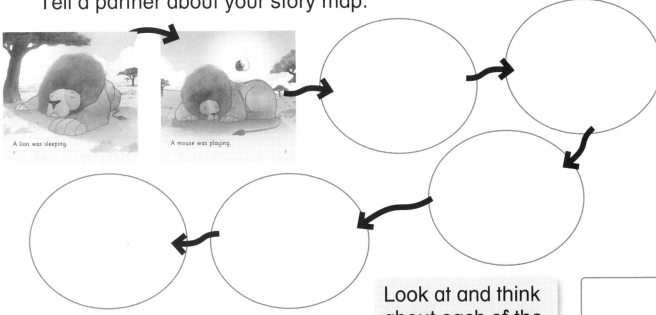

A lion was sleeping.

A mouse was playing.

Look at and think
about each of the
I can statements. ☐

Date: _____

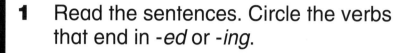

1   Read the sentences. Circle the verbs that end in *-ed* or *-ing*.

a Penguin is swimming with his friends in the water.

b Penguin climbed up the hill.

c Penguin jumped up into the air.

d Penguin is walking through the snow.

2   Complete the sentences. Use the words in the box.

running	sliding	laughed	looked

a Penguin _____ everywhere for his friends.

b Penguin is _____ through the snow.

c Penguin is _____ on the ice.

d Penguin _____ and played with his friends in the water.

3   Copy the sentences. Add a full stop (.), a question mark (?) or an exclamation mark (!) at the end of each sentence.

a Who is walking in the snow

_____

b Penguin looks down into the sea

_____

c SPLASH

_____

4 Read aloud the pages based on the story *The Lonely Penguin*.

It's Penguin. He's lonely. He's looking for his friends.

Crunch crunch! Penguin's walking in the snow.

Now he's climbing up the hill. Can he see his friends?

Penguin is swimming with his friends in the cold water.

5 Answer the questions. Tick the correct answers.

a Look at picture **1**. How does Penguin feel?

☐ lonely   ☐ happy

b Why does he feel like this?

☐ He is cold.   ☐ His friends are not with him.

c Look at picture **2**. What sound does he make as he walks in the snow?

_____

d Look at picture **3**. Where is Penguin?

_____

e Look at picture **4**. What is Penguin doing?

_____

6 Read the story aloud. Use your voice and hands to show how the characters feel in the story.

Look at and think about each of the *I can* statements.

☐

Date: _____

1 Write the names.

_____   _____   _____

2 Add letters to make words that rhyme.

room   broom

hook   coo __

look   b __ __ k

keep   sl __ __ p

rainbow   wind __ __

pool   c __ __ __

blow   sl __ __

reel   p __ __ __

3 🎧 Listen and write the sentences you hear. Then read your
Audio 6 sentences aloud.

a _____

b _____

c _____

d _____

4 Make a story map of *The Lonely Penguin*. Complete the sentences about the pictures in the story map.

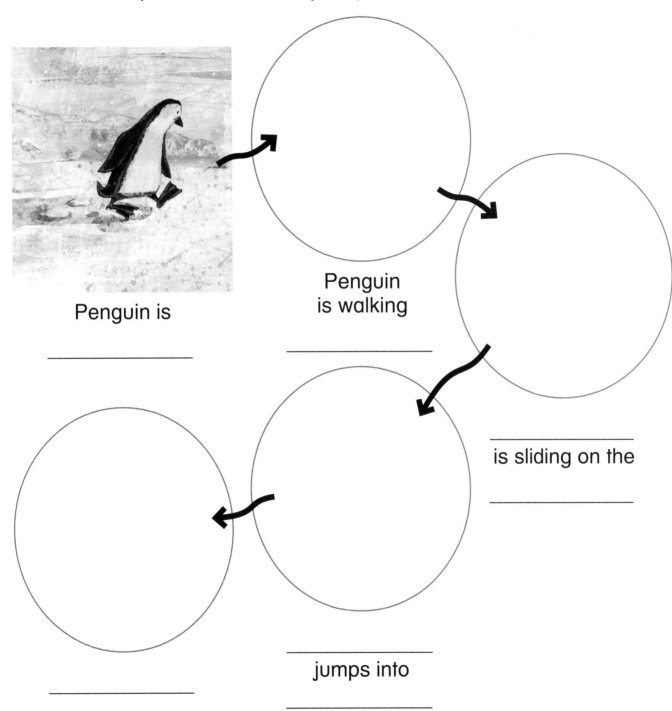

Penguin is

_____

Penguin
is walking

_____

_____

is sliding on the

_____

jumps into

_____

_____

_____

5 Retell the story of *The Lonely Penguin*. Use the sentences in your story map.

Look at and think about each of the *I can* statements.

Date: _____

1 Read the fact file about ostriches.

FACT FILE: Ostriches

Ostriches are birds that do not fly. They can be black and white or grey.

They live on dry land.

They eat small plants and insects. They do not have teeth so they eat small stones to help them swallow food.

Ostriches have two strong legs. They can run very fast.

Baby ostriches hatch from big eggs.

2 Copy three sentences that are true.

Ostriches are big birds.

Ostriches can fly.

Ostriches have long legs and they can run fast.

Ostriches lay eggs.

_____

_____

_____

3 Answer the questions.

a What colour are ostriches?

_____

b What do ostriches eat?

_____

c Where do ostriches live?

_____

d Why do ostriches eat small stones? Tick the correct answer.

☐ To clean their teeth. ☐ To help them swallow food.

4 What do you like to read, fact files about animals or stories about animals?

_____

5 Write a sentence about a bird that you have seen.

_____

Look at and think about each of the *I can* statements.

☐

Date: _____

1 Read aloud the pages below based on the story *Anansi and Turtle*.

Next day, Anansi found an invitation in his mailbox. So he put on his best coat and hat and walked to the pond.

"Come down," shouted Turtle. "I have all your favourite foods – chicken, rice and peas, and sweet coconut drops."

2 Answer the questions.

a Who wrote the invitation?

_____

b What time was dinner?

_____

c Where was dinner?

_____

d What food was on the table? Make a list. Give it a heading.

_____   _____

_____   _____

e Find and write two verbs that end in *-ed*.

_____   _____

f Find and write two plural nouns that end in *-s*.

_____   _____

3 🎧 Audio 7 Listen and complete the sentences.

a There is a _____ on the book.

b _____ brother is very _____.

c "_____ did you not wait for me?" said Turtle.

4 Write the words in these sentences in the correct order.

a into the water.   Anansi jumped

_____

b his coat   He took   and hat off.

_____

c eat the food.   watched   Anansi   his friend

_____

5 Write the sentences correctly. Start each one with a capital letter. Write a full stop or a question mark at the end.

a anansi tricked turtle

_____

b can i join you for dinner

_____

c turtle set the table at the bottom of the pond

_____

d do you like rice and beans

_____

Look at and think about each of the *I can* statements.

Date: _____

1   Make lists of words that rhyme. Read the words aloud.

cry	mice	stew

2   Draw a picture of two things you like to eat. Complete the sentence. Use 'and' in the sentence.

I like to eat _____

3   Circle the nouns in the sentences. Underline the verbs.

a   "I washed my hands," said Turtle.

b   Anansi put on his coat and his hat.

c   Anansi filled his pockets with stones.

4 Make an invitation. Write and draw pictures.

Invitation

Please come to _____

To _____

Place _____

Date _____

Time _____

From _____

Look at and think about each of the *I can* statements.

Date: _____

1 Complete the sentences to tell the first part of the story of *Anansi and Turtle*.

One day Turtle visited his friend Anansi.

Anansi was _____

Turtle wanted dinner too.

Anansi _____ Turtle.

He told Turtle to _____.

But Turtle was very slow.

Anansi _____ before Turtle came back.

2 What happened next? Write the story.

So Turtle tricked Anansi.

_____

_____

_____

_____

_____

_____

_____

_____

3 Read your sentences aloud to a partner.

4 Tell a partner what you think about Anansi and Turtle.

- Did they behave well?
- Were they clever or silly?
- What would you have done?

5 Think about the stories and information texts you have read this year.

What did you enjoy most? Make a list.

_____

_____

_____

_____

_____

6 Why did you enjoy the stories and texts? Tick all the sentences you agree with.

☐ They made me laugh.

☐ I learned about interesting things.

☐ I like to read about animals.

☐ I learned about how people behave.

☐ I liked the pictures.

Look at and think about each of the *I can* statements. ☐

Date: _____

1 Look at the pictures from the story *Zog and Zebra* and talk about them.

Then listen carefully to the story.

Zog was zooming around in his flying ship. He had found a lovely planet.
"Just where I can have my lunch," said Zog.

2

Zog landed on the ground and looked around.

He was hungry so he got his picnic basket. "I will have lunch and then I will look around," said Zog.

3

Zog saw Zebra.
"I am Zog," said Zog.
"My name is Zebra," said Zebra.
"I like your stripes," said Zog. "Have some of my picnic."

4

After lunch Zog and Zebra went to play.
"Shall we play hide and seek?" asked Zebra.
"You hide and I will count to ten," said Zog.

5

Where are you?

Zebra hid in the trees. Zog looked for Zebra. His stripes made him hard to see.

6

Next Zog hid. He was very quiet and very still. What was that?

Zog saw the long grass shake and quiver. Something was hidden in it.

7

2 Answer the questions about *Zog and Zebra*.

  a Who are the characters in the story? Write their names.

   _____   _____

  b How did Zog get to the ground? Tick the correct answer.

   ☐ in a boat

   ☐ in a flying ship

  c Why did Zog get out his picnic basket? Tick the correct answer.

   ☐ He wanted to sleep.

   ☐ He wanted to eat lunch.

  d How did Zog behave when he saw Zebra? Circle a word.

   angry   friendly   sad   afraid

  e What game did Zog and Zebra play?

   _____

  f Why did Zebra hide in the trees?

   _____

  g Where did Zog hide?

   _____

3 Find words in the story and write them here.

  a Find two verbs.

   _____   _____

  b Find two nouns.

   _____   _____

4 What do you think was in the grass? What happened next to Zog and Zebra? Talk about this and then write the story.

_____

_____

_____

_____

_____

_____

_____

_____

_____

_____

_____

_____

_____

_____

_____

_____

_____

_____

_____

5 Draw a story map of your story of Zog and Zebra.

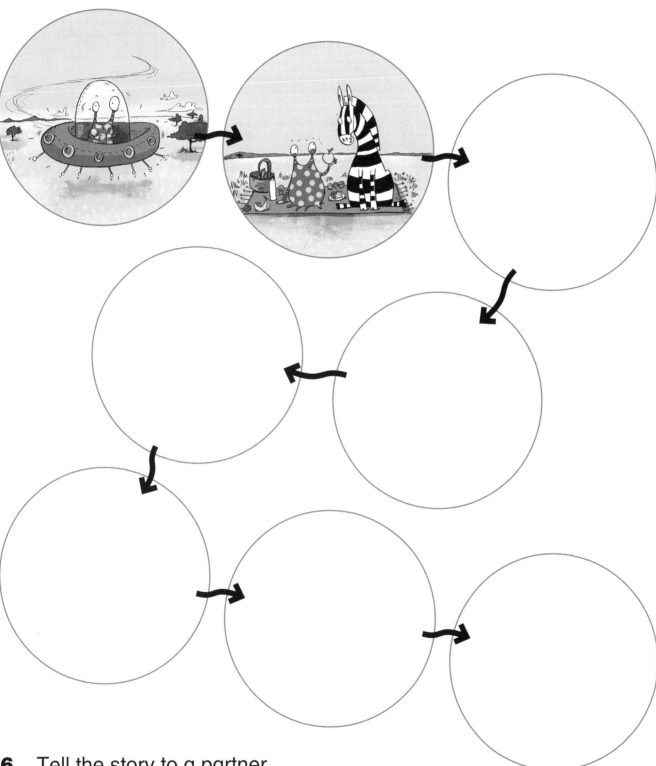

6 Tell the story to a partner.

Date: _____

Look at and think about each of the *I can* statements.

Acknowledgements

Text acknowledgements

The publishers gratefully acknowledge the permission granted to reproduce the copyright material in this book. Every effort has been made to trace copyright holders and to obtain their permission for the use of copyright material. The publishers will gladly receive any information enabling them to rectify any error or omission at the first opportunity.

Cover illustration: *The Lonely Penguin* Reprinted by permission of HarperCollins*Publishers* Ltd © 2011 Petr Horácek, *The Big Red Bus* Reprinted by permission of HarperCollins*Publishers* © 2006 Alison Hawes, illustrated by Woody Fox, *Pam Naps* Reprinted by permission of HarperCollins*Publishers* Ltd © 2011 Robyn Lever, illustrated by Tomislav Zlatic, *Up and Off!* Reprinted by permission of HarperCollins*Publishers* Ltd © 2019 Karra McFarlane, *Chick to Hen* Reprinted by permission of HarperCollins*Publishers* Ltd © 2011 Elspeth Graham, *Odd Fish!* Reprinted by permission of HarperCollins*Publishers* Ltd © 2020 Fiona Undrill, *Cubs* Reprinted by permission of HarperCollins*Publishers* Ltd © 2019 Sasha Morton, *Bot on the Moon* Reprinted by permission of HarperCollins*Publishers* Ltd © 2006 Shoo Rayner, *Funny Fish* Reprinted by permission of HarperCollins*Publishers* Ltd © 2005 Michaela Morgan, illustrated by Jon Stuart, *Red Hen* Reprinted by permission of HarperCollins*Publishers* Ltd © 2013 Pippa Goodhart, illustrated by Emily Carew Woodard, *The Small Bun* Reprinted by permission of HarperCollins*Publishers* Ltd © 2006 Martin Waddell, illustrated by T.S. Spookytooth, *The Lion and the Mouse* Reprinted by permission of HarperCollins*Publishers* Ltd © 2011 Anthony Robinson, illustrated by Ciaran Duffy, *The Lonely Penguin* Reprinted by permission of HarperCollins*Publishers* Ltd © 2011 Petr Horácek, *Zog and Zebra* Reprinted by permission of HarperCollins*Publishers* © 2013 Mal Peet and Elspeth Graham, illustrated by Sarah Horne.

Photo acknowledgements

The publishers gratefully acknowledge the permission granted to reproduce the copyright material in this book. Every effort has been made to trace copyright holders and to obtain their permission for the use of copyright material. The publishers will gladly receive any information enabling them to rectify any error or omission at the first opportunity.

P17c Mikolajn/Shutterstock; p24l David Chapman/Alamy Stock Photo; p24r imageBROKER/Alamy Stock Photo; p25l Jay Gao/Shutterstock; p25r Ondrej Prosicky/Shutterstock; p27tl David Steele/Shutterstock; p27tr Dr. Juergen Bochynek/Shutterstock; p27bl RuslanKphoto/Shutterstock; p27br Grace Wangui/Shutterstock; p28t David Denby Photography/Shutterstock; p30 Volodymyr Burdiak/Shutterstock; p31t Graham Taylor/Shutterstock; p31c Karen Gaabucayan/Shutterstock; p31b Egor Vlasov/Shutterstock; p32t Avalon/Photoshot License/Alamy Stock Photo; p32c Juniors Bildarchiv GmbH/Alamy Stock Photo; p32b Wild At Art/Shutterstock; p60tl Nattika/Shutterstock; p60tr T.Lagerwall/Shutterstock; p60bl Max Maier/Shutterstock; p60br Garsya/Shutterstock; p66t Radek Borovka/Shutterstock; p66cl Sergei25/Shutterstock; p66cr Jaroen Jaikla/Shutterstock; p66bl Paula French/Shutterstock; p66br Wirestock Creators/Shutterstock.